ANNE
HUTCHINSON
PURITAN PROTESTER

ANNE
HUTCHINSON
PURITAN PROTESTER

by Darlene R. Stille

Content Adviser: Len Travers, Ph.D.,
Department of History,
University of Massachusetts, Dartmouth

Reading Adviser: Rosemary G. Palmer, Ph.D.,
Department of Literacy, College of Education,
Boise State University

COMPASS POINT BOOKS ✦ MINNEAPOLIS, MINNESOTA

Compass Point Books
3109 West 50th Street, #115
Minneapolis, MN 55410

Visit Compass Point Books on the Internet at *www.compasspointbooks.com*
or e-mail your request to *custserv@compasspointbooks.com*

Editor: Julie Gassman
Page Production: Heather Griffin
Photo Researcher: Svetlana Zhurkin
Cartographer: XNR Productions, Inc.
Library Consultant: Kathleen Baxter

Art Director: Jaime Martens
Creative Director: Keith Griffin
Editorial Director: Carol Jones
Managing Editor: Catherine Neitge

Dedicated to Robert and Ruth Long. D.R.S.

Library of Congress Cataloging-in-Publication Data
Stille, Darlene R.
  Anne Hutchinson: Puritan protester / by Darlene R. Stille.
    p. cm.—(Signature lives)
  Includes bibliographical references and index.
  ISBN 0-7565-1577-7 (hard cover)
  1. Hutchinson, Anne Marbury, 1591–1643—Juvenile literature. 2. Puritan
women—Massachusetts—Biography—Juvenile literature. 3. Puritans—
Massachusetts—Biography—Juvenile literature. 4. Massachusetts—
History—Colonial period, ca. 1600–1775—Juvenile literature. I. Title. II.
Series.
  F67.H92S75 2006
  973.2'2092—dc22   2005025093

Signature Lives

COLONIAL AMERICA

As they arrived in North America, European colonists found an expansive land of potential riches and unlimited opportunities. Many left their homes in the Old World seeking religious and political freedom. Others sought the chance to build a better life for themselves. The effort to settle a vast territory was not easy, and the colonists faced struggles over land, religion, and freedoms. But despite the many conflicts, great cities emerged, new industries developed, and the foundation for a new type of government was laid. Meanwhile, Native Americans fought to keep their ancestral lands and traditions alive in a rapidly changing world that became as new to them as it was to the colonists.

Table of Contents

1 FOLLOWING HER CONSCIENCE

❦

It was a bitter cold day in November 1637. Anne Hutchinson stood in the chilly air of the meeting-house in what is now Cambridge, Massachusetts. It was a drafty building made of timbers cut from the surrounding forests. Clay was stuffed into the cracks to keep out the wind, but there was no fireplace to warm the air. Hutchinson was a woman of strong faith, with an independent streak that had caused trouble for the colony's founders.

In front of her at a table sat John Winthrop, governor of Massachusetts Bay Colony, wearing a black coat and ruffled white collar. His eyes looked sternly out above his neatly-trimmed gray beard. On rough benches behind Winthrop sat eight men dressed in black robes. They were Puritan ministers

A painting from the 1800s illustrates the courtroom scene from Anne Hutchinson's trial.

from nearby churches. Taking up all of the seats on the benches were 40 male judges. Hutchinson's friends, family, and other supporters had to stand in the back of the room.

Hutchinson, an ordinary-looking 46-year-old woman, was on trial for believing and preaching beliefs that did not follow the teachings of the Puritan church. At the time, there was no guaranteed right of religious freedom in the New World. In fact, the laws of Massachusetts did not allow its citizens to question the beliefs or practices of the Puritan faith. The governor and ministers felt Hutchinson was a threat to their way of life. Governor Winthrop even feared that the devil had given her power to set up a "community of women" that would work to spread "wickedness" throughout the colony.

Driven by her intense faith, Hutchinson had begun having meetings in her home, for both women and men, to discuss the Bible and its teachings. She believed that God could speak directly to anyone and did not communicate only through ministers. The popularity of her message was perceived as dangerous by the government and the clergy.

She was following in her father's footsteps. Anne's father was a minister in the Church of England, also known as the Anglican Church, but he openly opposed some of its practices. Anglican officials saw Puritans and ministers like Anne's father as a threat to their power in English society. Church officials did all they could to silence the Puritans. Many Puritans eventually fled from England to Holland, where the government was more tolerant,

Puritans were often ridiculed in public.

or to the North American wilderness.

Three years before her trial, Anne Hutchinson and her family made the difficult journey from England to Massachusetts Bay Colony so they could more freely practice their Puritan faith. Yet, now she faced a trial by the Puritans in the colony. The laws there were based on Puritan laws and rules, which were based on the Bible. The Puritan leaders believed that obeying these laws and rules was necessary to protect the colony and keep everyone safe in the wilderness. Hutchinson, however, believed that she had the right to disagree. The Puritans banished Hutchinson from Massachusetts Bay Colony, but they could not silence her.

Her family and 65 of her followers left Massachusetts. Hutchinson's beliefs led her to become one of the founding members of what is now Rhode Island, the first American colony to allow religious freedom. Hutchinson had much in common with Rhode Island's founder, Roger Williams. He too had been banned from Massachusetts by the Puritan colonial leaders for his belief that people should be free to practice the religion they choose. He also believed that the colonists did not have the right to take land from the Native Americans. Hutchinson agreed with Williams about respecting the Indians' right to their land. This belief caused further conflict with the colonial government.

In a time when questioning the government could lead to beatings, imprisonment, and banishment into the wilderness, Hutchinson was not afraid to stand up for beliefs that did not follow the government's teachings. She was one of the first people in North America to protest the policies of a government, a tradition that continues as a right of Americans today. ℘

The founder of Rhode Island, Roger Williams, welcomed settlers of all religions to his colony.

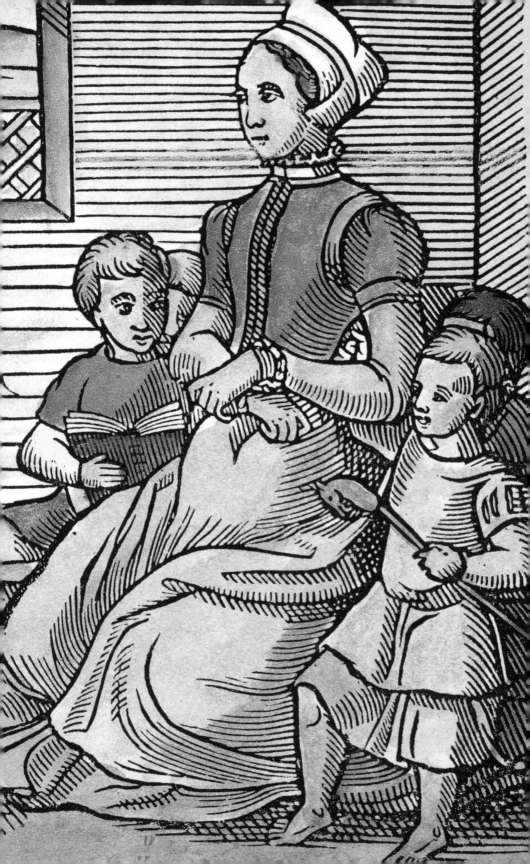

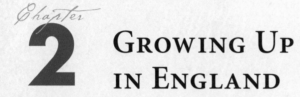

2 GROWING UP IN ENGLAND

❧⟨✦⟩❧

Anne Hutchinson's principles and bold actions were shaped in great part by her upbringing. She was born Anne Marbury in 1591 in Alford, England. There are no records of her birth date, but she was baptized on July 20, 1591. Alford was a little village of less than 500 people in the English countryside, about 140 miles (224 kilometers) from London. Anne's father, Francis Marbury, was a minister in the local Anglican church. Her mother, Bridget, was a midwife and helped women give birth.

The Rev. Francis Marbury was often in conflict with Anglican Church officials. He had been educated at Cambridge University, 50 miles (80 km) from London. At the university, there were many Puritan teachers. Puritans believed

> *Alford is located in Lincolnshire, a county near the eastern coast of England. Lincolnshire features varied terrain. In addition to flat and hilly land, there are also open areas called the heath where small, scrubby evergreens grow. Close to the sea-coast, there are large areas of low-lying wet-lands called marshes and fens.*

that ministers needed a college education to preach sermons that would help church members in their religious life. The Puritan teachers viewed sermons as the most important part of a worship service. Marbury came away from Cambridge with this belief as well, although he did not consider himself a Puritan.

As an Anglican minister, however, Marbury criticized the ministers who had little or no education. He also criticized the bishops who appointed them. He believed, as he had been trained by his teachers, that the church had a duty to be sure its ministers had a proper education. How could they preach to a congregation if they did not know what they were talking about? Marbury accused the bishops of "killing" souls because they appointed incompetent ministers.

Marbury was not shy about sharing his views. He often scolded the church for its policies, and his bishop arrested him twice for religious trouble-making. He served time in jail, but upon release he started criticizing the bishop again. In 1578, the bishop sent Marbury to St. Paul's Cathedral in London to be tried for failing to conform to Anglican practices. Although Marbury was accused of being a Puritan, he believed that he was a loyal Anglican Church minister who simply wanted the clergy to be well educated. But the church court convicted him and sent him to prison for two years.

When the two years were over, church officials hoped that Marbury's time in prison had taught him a lesson and that he would stop criticizing the church. After his release, the bishop assigned him to a parish in the little town of Alford. Marbury earned an additional small income by teaching at a local school

The original St. Paul's Cathedral, where Marbury's trial was held, was destroyed during London's Great Fire of 1666. It was rebuilt in a different style.

As a boy, *Captain John Smith, a famous English soldier and explorer, attended the school where Anne Hutchinson's father taught. In 1607, Smith helped found the Jamestown colony in Virginia. In 1614, he explored the coast of Massachusetts, where Anne Hutchinson would settle. He named the area New England.*

for poor boys. Marbury and Bridget Dryden married several years later in about 1588.

When Anne was born in 1591, her father was again in trouble with the church. This time he did not have to go to jail, but he was forbidden from preaching or teaching for several years. He had to stay home and farm his land. Most people who lived outside of big cities in England in the 1500s owned some land, and if they did not farm crops, they at least kept a big garden.

From the time she was a young child, Anne helped her parents with the household chores. Her mother also showed her how to be a midwife and often took her along to help with births. In those days, women did not go to hospitals to deliver their babies. They had their babies at home, and many women relied on midwives to help them. Midwives possessed many skills to help women have a safe delivery, but often there were problems with the baby, and the child would be stillborn. Many women died in childbirth from blood loss or infection. In fact, Francis Marbury's first wife, Elizabeth, had died after delivering her third child.

A midwife helps a woman deliver her baby in an illustration from the 16th century.

Bridget was Francis' second wife, and Anne was the second oldest of their 15 children. Anne helped her mother with her younger brothers and sisters and did chores around the house. There was always much work to do in a country household in England in the 1600s. There were animals to feed and care for, butter to churn, candles and soap to make, and wool to spin into yarn for clothing. Children began helping with the chores as soon as they could walk and talk, and they did not have much time to play. Adults did not view childhood as a separate or special time of life. They saw children as just being small adults and even dressed them in the kind of clothing adults wore, only in smaller sizes.

When Anne was old enough, her father taught her how to read. She was an eager student, and her parents were excellent teachers. Girls in those days were not allowed to attend school. At the time, most

A drawing from the mid-1600s shows a typical scene in rural England.

women in England could not read or write. Many men believed that girls and women had weak minds. They thought that education could harm a woman by weakening her physically, or even driving her mad.

All of the Marbury children learned to read by using three texts. They read the Bible, a popular book about martyred Christian saints, and a play script that their father wrote about his trial in 1578. He loved to tell his children about his trial. He was the hero in this story, and he poked fun at the bishop who led the trial. He told how he stood up to the bishop. He argued and quoted the Bible and gave clever answers to the bishop's questions. The play claimed that he had not been afraid because he believed he was innocent and God was on his side.

Anne's father taught her more than just how to read. He taught her how to think for herself. She learned how to reason and how to argue a case. Anne did not fear ministers or bishops, and she often listened to her father and his friends talk about theology, the study of God and religious beliefs. She memorized much of the Bible and came to have a deep faith in God. Like her father, she was ready to defend her faith. She was ready to stand up for what she believed—no matter what. ✒

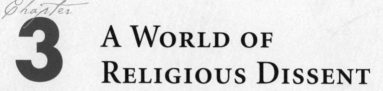

3 A WORLD OF RELIGIOUS DISSENT

❧⟨∾⟩❧

Religious trouble began brewing in Europe before Anne—and even her father—was born. In 1517, a German priest named Martin Luther protested what he saw as abuses and corruption in the Catholic Church. Luther's protests led to a religious movement called the Reformation and a new kind of Christianity called Protestantism.

At that time, all governments in Europe had an official, or state, religion. Before the Reformation, Catholicism was the state religion of all Christian countries in western Europe. This meant the pope and other church officials held political power, alongside kings, dukes, and other rulers. This was true in England, until the reign of Henry VIII.

King Henry, a practicing Catholic, wanted a

Martin Luther was angered by the sale of indulgences, or pardons for the penalty of sins, by Catholic Church officials. He began the Protestant movement and founded the Lutheran church.

divorce from his wife, Catherine of Aragon. Catherine bore six children, but only their daughter Mary had lived. Henry wanted a male heir for the throne, and for that, he thought he needed a new wife. The pope refused to grant Henry a divorce, so in 1533 Henry declared England independent of the Catholic Church.

Henry VIII introduces Anne Boleyn to the English court in an 18th-century painting.

He established the Protestant Anglican Church, or Church of England, as the official church and named himself the head. Then he divorced Catherine and married Anne Boleyn, who had a daughter, Elizabeth. He had Anne beheaded, and his next wife finally bore him a son. In all, Henry had six wives and three children that lived.

After Henry's death, his 9-year-old son became King Edward VI. When Edward died at age 15, his half sister, Mary, daughter of Catherine, became queen. She was a devout Catholic and restored the Catholic Church as the official religion in England. Anyone who did not worship as a Catholic was punished or put to death. So many Protestants were burned at the stake that the queen became known as "Bloody Mary."

When Mary died, Elizabeth, Henry VIII's second eldest daughter, was crowned queen. Elizabeth restored the Church of England as the nation's official religion, but like her father, she left many rituals the same as in the Catholic Church.

Many Anglican ministers wanted those Catholic rites and rituals removed from the Church of England. They thought services should emphasize Scripture, per-

Elizabeth I ruled England from 1558 until 1603. This time is called the Elizabethan Age. Elizabeth was a clever politician and a skillful ruler. She was able to keep both Catholic and Protestant subjects loyal to her. During her reign, Britain became a major European power.

The Anglican Church kept the look and feel of the Roman Catholic Church. The churches featured altars and crucifixes and were decorated with gold and gems. The traditional services were filled with music and grand rituals, and members celebrated Holy Communion, as they had as Roman Catholics.

sonal prayer, and sermons, not music, sacraments, and memorized prayer. These ministers and their followers who hoped to "purify" the church came to be called Puritans.

Anne's father, who was born in 1556, was embroiled in this world of religious dissent. As a member of the Marbury household, Anne listened to all the arguments about differences in beliefs. She heard ministers quote parts of the Bible to defend their beliefs. Her father also used the Bible to show why ministers needed to be well educated.

But with a growing family to support, Francis Marbury also needed to make a living. He depended on his work as a minister and preacher in a church. So he gave up openly criticizing the Anglican bishops and kept his opinions to himself. His silence helped improve his position within the church. One day in 1605, Marbury had news to tell his family. He had been given a job at a church in London. The whole family was moving to the capital of England, where its kings and queens lived. The Marburys would live in a house attached to the church—St. Martin in the Vintry. Anne was 14 at the time.

All of their friends in Alford would miss them,

An illustration from the mid-1600s compared Anglican and Puritan services.

but a boy named William Hutchinson was particularly sad to see Anne go. Will, the son of a well-to-do cloth merchant, was five years older than Anne. He knew her from attending Sunday church services. Sometimes he also saw her on Tuesdays and Fridays, Alford's market days, when vendors came to sell their wares of baked goods, flowers, fish, and vegetables.

Will worked in his father's textile shop, which provided him with the excuse of making trips to London to buy cloth. The trip took three days on horseback, but Will did not mind because at the end

A late 16th-century engraving of London

of the journey was a lively, brilliant young woman. Anne was quite different from this quiet, easygoing young man.

The London that Will traveled to was very different from sleepy little Alford. Anne's home was about a block from the banks of the River Thames, where ships sailed to and from distant lands. About a quarter of a mile away was the famous Tower of London, where Anne Boleyn had been beheaded. Just across the river was the Globe theater, where William Shakespeare was writing and acting in plays.

But Anne and her family didn't go to the theater. Their entertainment came in the form of gathering to read Bible passages in the evenings. They studied every word of every verse and debated among themselves about what each passage might mean. Anne had a talent for interpreting the Bible. If she had been a boy, she might have attended Cambridge University and become a Puritan preacher. But Anne was a woman, and no woman in England in the 1600s could even think about this kind of a life. ☙

Puritans did not attend frivolous entertainment like Shakespeare's plays. They thought such plays were lewd and corrupt. (And they often were!) In 1644, the Puritans had the Globe theater torn down.

They shall be ... of God and ... Christ

4 LOVE AND MARRIAGE

Chapter

❦

In 1611, Anne's father died at the age of 55, and her family lost their home in London. They had to leave the house in the church to make room for the new minister and his family.

William took the opportunity to ask Anne, now 20 years old, to marry him, and she accepted. This tall, reserved man and his bright, fiery bride were wed in August 1612. The newlyweds made their home in a small cottage back in Alford, where the Hutchinson family textile business was located.

As newlyweds, the young couple liked to visit churches in nearby towns. Almost every Sunday, they walked or rode their horse to "seek after the Lord of Hosts." Then one day, they heard about a new preacher who would change their lives. His name

The Reverend John Cotton (1584–1652) was an important spiritual leader for Anne Hutchinson.

was John Cotton.

Cotton was named the vicar of St. Boltoph's church in Boston, England, the same year that Anne and Will were married. Boston was a busy seaport on the Witham River, about 24 miles (38 km) from Alford. Cotton, like Anne's father, had been educated at Cambridge University.

One Sunday, Anne and Will decided to make the

St. Boltoph's Church in Boston, England, as it appears today

journey to Boston to hear Cotton's preaching for themselves. They got up before dawn and rode for six hours on horseback to the huge Boston church. It was a journey that changed Hutchinson's life.

Hundreds of people stood in the church as Cotton, dressed in a plain black robe with white collar and tabs, climbed the steps to the church's magnificent pulpit. Everyone listened intently as he preached for hours. Anne was spellbound. She had never heard anything like his preaching.

> *St. Boltoph's Church in Boston, England, dates from the Middle Ages. Work began on the building in 1309. A huge, 272-foot (83-meter) square tower sits on top of the building and gives the church its nickname, "the Boston Stump." The tower is so tall that it can be seen from 20 miles (32 km) away.*

John Cotton preached a fiery message that said that all people were born sinners and could be saved, or go to heaven, only by the grace of God. According to Puritan belief, there was nothing human beings could do to save themselves from their sins, and no amount of good works could earn God's forgiveness. God had to forgive and save them by an act of his grace.

Some Puritan ministers taught that people had to obey the laws of the church to show they were saved by grace. Although Cotton thought it was important to follow church laws, he did not believe that doing so was the only way one could be saved. Puritans called going to church and obeying religious laws "works." They argued all the time about which was more important, works or grace. Anne was sure that Cotton was right about the importance of grace. She thought that he was the best of all the Puritan preachers.

Anne and William attended Cotton's church as often as they could. After they started their family, they hitched up a horse and wagon and the whole family set off for Boston. Their first child was born in 1613. The baby boy, named Edward, was a great joy to the Hutchinsons, who loved children.

They were destined to have a very large family, just like Anne's parents. In fact, a new baby was born about every 18 months for the next 23 years. The Hutchinsons would eventually have 15 children that lived beyond infancy. The sounds of young children laughing and playing, along with a baby crying, always filled the Hutchinson home. Raising this large family and running an efficient household took a great deal of effort and good management skills. Fortunately, Will was doing well in the textile business, and the family was able to afford servants to help with household chores. Also, as in all large families of that time, Anne's older children, under her guidance and supervision, helped care for the younger ones.

Because of the help she got from her servants and older children, Hutchinson was able to use her

*Many Puritan
women were
educated in
order to read
the Bible.*

boundless energy and intelligence for other activities.
She became a highly skilled midwife like her mother,
helping women with their childbirth. She planted an
herb garden and used the herbs to make medicines.
Hutchinson also made time for her greatest passion—
reading and interpreting the Bible.

Cotton's teachings became a very important part
of Hutchinson's life. She wanted to spread the word

about his belief in the importance of grace. So she began holding weekly meetings for women in her Alford home. She passed along Cotton's teachings, discussed the Sunday sermon, and studied Bible passages. Hutchinson and Cotton became friends. They worked as a team to spread his view of God's grace.

When the Hutchinsons could not make the journey to Boston, they often attended church in the nearby village of Bilsby. John Wheelwright, their brother-in-law, was the minister there. He had married Will's sister Mary in 1629. Wheelwright was also a Puritan, and Anne said he was the best preacher after Cotton. The two couples became close friends.

The Reverend John Wheelwright (1592–1679)

For 18 years, the Hutchinsons were happy. They loved loading their growing family into a wagon and going to Boston to hear Cotton's sermons. Other Sundays were spent with the Wheelwrights. As the Hutchinson children grew older, they too came to see Cotton as a great teacher and preacher. And Anne's weekly meetings, where she taught and preached to the local women, left her feeling very rewarded.

But in the summer of 1630, their world began to change. First, the plague struck Alford.

Outbreaks of plague have killed millions of people since ancient times. In the 1300s, a huge outbreak called the Black Death killed about one-third of the people in Europe. After that, there were smaller outbreaks from time to time. It is now known that the plague is caused by a germ, or bacterium, that infects rats and other rodents. Fleas that bite the rodents pass the germ along when they bite humans. In 1630, however, no one in Alford, or most of England, knew what caused the plague or how to treat it.

To ward it off, they tried making loud noises and ringing the church bell. They bathed less often than usual, which was never more than once a month. They sniffed pleasant odors in hopes of driving the plague away. Anne Hutchinson went from one sick person to another, doing all she could to help. However, once people fell ill with fever or red blotches on their skin, they usually died within a few days. Two of Hutchinson's daughters—Elizabeth, a teenager,

Today, doctors cure people who catch the plague with antibiotic drugs. Although there are very few cases of plague today, it is still a serious illness. Unless it is treated within five days, the victim could die.

and Susanna, who was only about 8 years old—died in the outbreak. Hutchinson was heartbroken. She stayed in her home and grieved. She could not bring herself to serve as a midwife, visit the market, or even attend church. She saw hardly anyone aside from her family for about a year.

Meanwhile, the Church of England was determined to stamp out Puritanism. The Wheelwrights had to flee Bilsby in 1632 and go into hiding to keep Anglican Church officials from putting John in jail. To escape persecution, many Puritans decided to leave England for Holland or the great wilderness of North America. John Cotton decided to flee before he was sent to jail. In 1633, he and some of his followers boarded a ship called the *Griffin* and set sail for the new Massachusetts Bay Colony in North America.

Hutchinson was devastated. She had lost two great spiritual friends—her brother-in-law, John Wheelwright, and her minister and teacher, John Cotton. Her oldest son, Edward, then 20 years old, had also decided to leave England for Massachusetts and sailed with Cotton.

Hutchinson could not rest until she followed them to the New World. She was willing to leave her friends and her comfortable cottage in Alford. But she was not willing to leave her family. Ten of her

The Church of England became even more anti-Puritan in 1633, when William Laud (1573–1645) was named archbishop of the Anglican Church in Canterbury.

children—Richard, Faith, Bridget, Francis, Samuel, Anne, Mary, Katherine, William, and Susanna— were still living in England. Richard was about 18 years old, but Susanna (named after her deceased sister) was just an infant. Hutchinson persuaded her husband and children that they should all follow Edward and their beloved teacher to the new land. There they would have the freedom to practice their religion and live in peace—or so they thought. ॐ

Chapter

5 A NEW HOME IN A NEW WORLD

❧

In the summer of 1634, Anne Hutchinson and her family boarded the *Griffin*, the same wooden sailing ship on which Cotton and her son had traveled the year before. In the 1630s, setting out across the North Atlantic Ocean was a dangerous adventure. Ships were not built to carry passengers then. The *Griffin*, like all other oceangoing ships, was made to carry cargo. With no rooms specifically built to be living quarters, passengers fit in wherever they could. They slept on simple wooden bunks or on hammocks slung between the ceiling beams.

The *Griffin* could carry about 200 passengers. However, John Winthrop, the governor of Massachusetts Bay Colony, had asked that some cattle be brought on the next ship sailing to the colony.

A ship traveling across the Atlantic Ocean struggled against a harrowing storm.

So, the 12 Hutchinsons journeyed with about 90 other passengers and a herd of cows and other farm animals.

Even though they were heading off to build homes in the wilderness, the Puritan families could not take very much with them. Among the items they packed were tools, weapons, bedding, warm clothes, pots, and kettles. They also brought some furniture, including chairs, benches, tables, and cabinets.

An early 17th-century cabinet is typical of the type of furniture Puritans brought with them from England.

Once their belongings were stowed in the hold of the ship, Anne and her family stepped aboard. Searchers came aboard as well, to see who the emigrants were. These British government officials checked to see that the passengers' papers were in order and made them swear an oath of loyalty to the English government. But they let the Puritans leave England for the New World.

The Hutchinsons climbed down a ladder to a space below the wooden deck. It was dark and crowded, and damp from seawater that had seeped in. It smelled terrible. This was their home for the two months it took to sail across the Atlantic.

A seaborne ship did not make a comfortable home. Seasickness, caused by the constant motion of the water, could last for weeks.

In addition, storms were a great danger for voyagers on the sea. There was no way to predict the weather much in advance. When sailors saw waves building up, they knew a storm with fierce winds was coming and it was time to take down the sails. The little ship would bob about in the stormy seas

Around 20,000 English men, women, and children left Europe to come to the New World between 1620 and 1643. Making the difficult journey across 3,000 miles (4,800 km) of ocean was a tremendous challenge during the much less advanced 17th century. One historian compared it "to the effort it would require today to transport the two million people of Phoenix, Arizona, to the moon and establish a colony there."

like a cork on the water. Passengers went below the deck and hung on as the ship rolled and bounced in the waves. If they were not careful, they could bang their heads on low beams.

Fourteen years earlier, another group of Puritans called Pilgrims had made the same journey in a similar ship called the *Mayflower*. One of the

A storm tossed the Mayflower *so much that a beam bowed and cracked. Passengers were able to repair the leaky crack.*

Pilgrims told of a man who ventured up on deck during a storm:

> *In a mighty storm, a lusty young man called John Howland, coming upon some occasion above the gratings was, with a roll of the ship, thrown into the sea, but it pleased God that he caught hold of the topsail halyards [ropes] which hung over-board. ... He held his hold ... till he was hauled up by the same rope to the brim of the water, and then with a boat hook and other means got into the ship.*

Boredom was another problem on sea voyages in the 1600s. During fair weather, passengers could spend some time on deck. Each day's activities were much the same. They awakened, put away their bedding, and then said prayers. Next they ate a simple breakfast. With no refrigeration, they had to carry food that would not spoil easily. The most common foods on a sea voyage were dried and salted meat and fish, peas

The Pilgrims were a group of Puritans. There was a difference, however, between the Pilgrims and other Puritans. While both the Puritans and Pilgrims felt the Anglican religion was too much like the Roman Catholic Church, Puritans still thought of themselves as members of the Church of England. They simply wanted to change the church. The Pilgrims, however, left the Church of England and started their own religion. Pilgrims first fled England for Holland, where they were allowed religious freedom. Then in 1620, they took their famous journey in the Mayflower to the New World.

Until the late 1700s, sailors and passengers on long sea voyages were in danger of getting a disease called scurvy, which was caused by a lack of vitamin C. The disease weakened the walls of their blood vessels and other body cells. The sailors bruised easily, their gums bled, and their teeth fell out. Often death followed. People knew that eating fresh foods helped scurvy, but they did not know which foods worked best. In the mid-1700s, a doctor in the British Navy found that citrus fruits were the best foods to treat or prevent scurvy. The British Navy began giving sailors lime or lemon juice every day. As a result, few British sailors developed scurvy.

and beans, and hard cheese.

Sometimes the women cooked food for the midday meal. But they had to wait for the working sailors to finish using the ship's simple stove. The hardworking sailors felt they needed a hot meal each day, but the Puritans did not. After all, the passengers were only sitting around.

Hutchinson had a great deal of time to read the Bible, pray, and think during the long voyage to Massachusetts Bay Colony. Her belief in God was deeply personal, and she believed God spoke to her. During the long days at sea, she listened for revelations from God. She was sure that God had revealed to her the day on which they would arrive in the New World.

The long days at sea were good opportunities for ministers to preach. They held worship services every day and preached sermons that often lasted several hours. One August afternoon as the ship rose and fell with the waves, Hutchinson listened intently to a sermon by a minister named Zechariah Symmes. She and Symmes had met just before the *Griffin* sailed, and they did not seem to like one another. Symmes thought Hutchinson was "corrupt and narrow." For four hours, he preached about the importance of love for one's neighbor. He advised that neighborly love was favorable as a:

> *... means of evidencing a good spiritual estate. In our love we will "grow in grace," for we must strive always to lay up a "stock of grace."*

Hutchinson was troubled by the sermon. She believed that grace came only from God and there was no way to "stock" it up. During the question period after the sermon, she spoke up and accused Symmes of preaching false truths. "Your words bear a legal savor, and they do not correspond with my understanding on the doctrine," she said.

Symmes reminded her that women were never to

A rare drawing of Anne Hutchinson created after her lifetime

A windmill overlooks early houses at the settlement of Boston in Massachusetts Bay Colony.

speak out during a worship service, using a Bible passage to make his point: "For the man is not of the woman, but the woman of the man."

The two then got into a loud argument. Hutchinson saw nothing wrong with her actions. After all, disagreeing with ministers was normal in the home where she grew up. Because she believed he was entirely wrong, Hutchinson threatened to tell the other colonists in Massachusetts Bay all about Symmes' false beliefs. Symmes replied with his own threat of reporting her to colony officials upon their arrival.

Then Hutchinson told the minister that God revealed future events to her and actually predicted the day the ship would arrive at Massachusetts Bay Colony. "What would you say if we should be at New England within these three weeks?"

People who claimed to know the future were viewed with suspicion, and Symmes refused to believe that God would speak to her. After that, Hutchinson ignored Symmes. She told other women on the ship to ignore him, too.

The *Griffin* did land at Massachusetts Bay Colony on the day that Anne had predicted— September 18, 1634. Symmes was not impressed. He went straight to church authorities to report on Hutchinson's "awful" behavior. Symmes said that Hutchinson should not be allowed to join the church because she criticized the ministers. John Cotton was called upon to vouch for Hutchinson. He assured everyone that she was a true believer and a good Puritan. Hutchinson joined the church in the new settlement called Boston. But she had made an enemy of Zechariah Symmes. ৯

6 Life in Massachusetts Bay Colony

Chapter

৵৵৵

Boston, Massachusetts, had been named for Boston, England, where many of the Puritans had lived. The Boston of the New World, however, looked nothing like the Boston they had left behind.

The sound of pounding hammers and the fresh smell of wood and sawdust filled the air as new houses rose up along muddy streets. The most important building in town was the new meeting-house where men came together to discuss the colony's business. The meetinghouse also served as the place where the congregation of the First Church of Boston met every Sunday.

Around the edge of the new town stood towering trees in a vast forest. The Hutchinsons had never seen anything like it. Some of the trees were hundreds of

Late 19th-century artisit, Howard Pyle, known as the Father of American Illustration, drew Anne Hutchinson preaching in her home.

years old. The Native Americans who lived in the forest had never needed to cut down the huge pines, oaks, and maples. The Puritans, however, cut down trees to clear the land for their farms and to get lumber for their houses.

When the Hutchinsons arrived in Massachusetts Bay, groups of Puritans had already established several settlements at Salem, Boston, Newtowne (now Cambridge), and other places that would become major cities in New England. Already, about 5,000 people were living in Massachusetts Bay Colony.

Roger Williams, the founder of Rhode Island, served as pastor of the church in Salem.

The first group to arrive was made up of Puritans who settled at Salem in 1626. A group of about 700 Puritans followed in 1630, with John Winthrop leading them, and they established what became Boston and Cambridge. Charles I, who was then king of England, gave the Puritans a charter, which gave them the right to take over these lands and set up Massachusetts Bay.

Governor John Winthrop (1588–1649)

This colony was a great dream of Governor Winthrop. He wanted to create a perfect settlement and build "a city on a hill." He believed the colony, its church, people, and government should be an example to the world. Winthrop was not a minister. He had been a lawyer in London. But he had a vision of a virtuous society built on a foundation of the Bible's teachings. All of the colony's laws would be based on the Bible and Puritan beliefs. Winthrop wanted the people in old England to see what a wonderful society the Puritans could make in the new England.

Winthrop had led these new settlers to

There were other colonies in the New World besides Massachusetts Bay Colony. The Spanish founded the first permanent settlement in North America at St. Augustine, Florida, in 1565. The first permanent English settlers arrived at Jamestown, Virginia, in 1607. The Dutch in 1624 set up a colony in what is now New York City. Swedish settlers established the colony of New Sweden in parts of Delaware and New Jersey in 1638.

Massachusetts Bay. He hired 11 ships to carry all of them and their belongings. They faced terrible hardships when they arrived at the settlement at Salem. The Salem settlers who had come before them did not have enough food, and there was no shelter for so many new people. A trapper told Winthrop the land was better at a place that is now the city of Boston.

The Puritans went there and camped out all winter in wigwams, huts, and caves. When spring came, they cleared enough of the forest to start building churches, homes, and farms. Almost 200 of the Puritans died the first year. A powerful belief that God was leading them helped the survivors keep going.

The Puritans saw life as a constant struggle between good and evil, between God and Satan. They believed God punished or rewarded people for their actions. Sin, they thought, was often punished by sickness. Wealth and other good fortune could be signs of God's favor. They also believed that storms or other natural disasters could be sent by God as a punishment for a community's wrongdoing.

Puritans believed that everyone was born a sinner and that God could save sinners by an act of grace. God, however, did not save everyone. He chose only a few people to save. The Puritans called the chosen

Many cities in the New World were established along shorelines to provide the communities with ports.

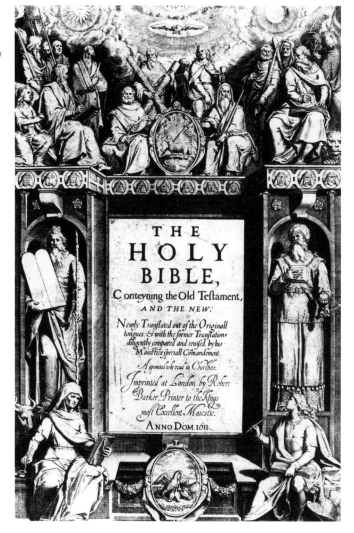

An elaborate illustration faced the title page of the King James Bible, published in 1611.

ones "the elect." Like followers of other religions, the Puritans believed that they were the only ones who knew how God wanted people to live.

They came to this conclusion after studying the Bible extensively. The Bible was in some ways a new book in the 1600s. Before the Reformation, only Catholic priests and educated men and women could read it, since it was written in Greek and Latin. Then in 1535, the first English Bible was printed, and the King James Version followed in 1611. Now Puritans could read the Bible in their own language.

They studied every word and tried to solve the Bible's mysteries. They studied the story of Moses, who led the ancient Israelites out of Egypt to the Promised Land. The Puritans compared themselves to the ancient Israelites and believed they were God's chosen people. He had led them out of England just as he led the Israelites out of Egypt. North America was their Promised Land.

Like all Puritans, the Hutchinsons were driven by their faith in God. As soon as they arrived in Boston, Will hired laborers to build a house for the family in the best area of town, right across from Governor Winthrop's house. The family also had a 600-acre (240-hectare) farm outside of town. Will had made a great deal of money in the textile business, so the Hutchinsons were one of the wealthiest new families in the colony.

Wealthy or not, life in the colony was hard for everyone, but it was especially hard on the women. Many women died from complications of childbirth. Poor nutrition and too much hard work in the fields and the home sent many women to their sickbeds.

Hutchinson was greatly concerned by the problems of the women colonists. She served as a midwife in Massachusetts just as she had in England. She soon became one of the most popular women in town. She held special status. Not only was she intelligent, kind, and outgoing, she was a personal friend of John Cotton.

Cotton had been hired as a teacher in the First Church of Boston. The regular minister, John Wilson, was away in England when the Hutchinsons arrived. Cotton filled in for him by preaching every Sunday and giving lectures during the week. He was one

Colonists spent much of their free time reading and studying the Bible.

of the most respected men in Massachusetts, and few people wanted to miss his sermons. Hutchinson once again could focus on the lessons that he taught. Now, she did not have to travel many miles to hear him. She lived in the same town.

Hutchinson's mind was filled with ideas on the Bible's teaching, and she wanted to share these ideas with others. She invited women to come to her home as she had in Alford. They began meeting once a week to talk about Cotton's sermon and Bible passages.

John Cotton was quite popular in the community. John Winthrop said "the Lord [gave] special testimony of His presence in the church of Boston, after Mr. Cotton was called to office there. More were converted and added to the church, than to all the other churches in the bay ..."

Hutchinson was an excellent speaker and teacher. She sat with the Bible open on a table in front of her. Her audience sat on benches and listened and asked questions. Because no one really knew if they were among God's chosen, they worried a lot about heaven and hell and what would happen to their souls after they died. Most Puritan ministers preached sermons that made them worry even more.

These ministers told them they must show that they were chosen by God to be among the elect. They could show this by performing works—obeying all the church rules and laws. If they were elect, they would listen to their ministers and never do anything wrong. People worried about their behavior. If they did or thought something "bad," would this mean they would not go to heaven when they died?

Hutchinson helped Puritan women feel better. She told them not to worry about church laws and that they should trust their inner feelings. They would be able to feel God's love like an inner light. She said, "As I understand it, laws, commands, rules and edicts are for those who have not the light which makes plain the pathway. "

Hutchinson's thinking about God's grace had begun to go beyond Cotton's beliefs. She thought up new ideas about grace and came to believe that God could speak directly to anyone. She thought that people could know the will of God and what was right if they looked deep within themselves and sought out a kind of "inner light." Works of any kind were totally unnecessary. She wanted to share her ideas about grace with others.

Every week, more and more women came to Hutchinson's meeting. Soon, some of the women brought their husbands. There were too many people to fit in her house, so she began to hold two meetings every week. Between 60 and 80 men and women came to each meeting.

From his house across the street, John Winthrop could see people coming and going from the Hutchinsons' house. He began to worry about the

Boston's first meetinghouse

influence she was having on the people of the colony. He wrote in his journal that more people went to her "for counsel about matters of conscience ... than any minister (I might say all the elders) in the country."

The next year, the Rev. John Wilson returned to Boston. He was not as good a preacher as Cotton, and he was not popular. In fact, many church members—including Anne Hutchinson—did not like him at all. Winthrop and other church members, however, liked him and his ideas. Wilson believed that the Puritans had to show they were the elect of God by obeying their ministers and all of the rules and laws. By 1635, a big disagreement broke out in the Massachusetts colony between those who supported the grace ideas of Hutchinson and those who supported the works ideas of Winthrop and Wilson. ℘

Chapter
7   TRIAL AND BANISHMENT

☗

The Puritans who followed Hutchinson's teachings believed that people could feel the love and presence of God in their hearts. They did not need ministers to tell them what God wanted of them, and they did not have to show their righteousness through works. Other Puritans, including most of the ministers, thought this was a dangerous, "do nothing" way of looking at life. They believed that people had to follow the laws and rules, go to church, and read the Bible for the common good of their righteous new society. They feared Hutchinson's dangerous teachings would lead to nothing but lawlessness and immorality. The ministers also wondered if there would even be a need for ministers if people followed their own "inner light."

Time in the stocks was a typical punishment for those who didn't follow the Puritan laws in Massachusetts Bay Colony.

Hutchinson and her followers came to be called Antinomians. Antinomianism is the belief that God does not require that people follow laws of Scripture, ethics, or morality, and that salvation is given only through God's grace. The title of Antinomian was an insult that implied that their beliefs were immoral.

This arguing upset Governor Winthrop. He wanted everyone in his colony to have the same beliefs and live together peacefully. What kind of example was the colony setting with all this arguing? People in England even heard about the problem. The king considered taking away their charter and sending a royal governor to rule them. Winthrop definitely did not want that.

In addition, there were enemies all around them. The French wanted land in North America. And despite the fact that the Indians had been peaceful, the English feared they could attack at any time. The colonists needed to be united for protection instead of split into two groups.

Winthrop believed that Hutchinson used her meetings to stir up trouble. He thought she was criticizing all ministers except John Cotton and John Wheelwright, who was now a pastor in a nearby community. Winthrop did not like Hutchinson. In his journal, he wrote that she was "a woman of a haughty and fierce carriage (a way of presenting herself), a nimble wit and an active spirit, and a very voluble tongue (fearless in speaking out)." In another journal entry, he called her an "American Jezebel," after an

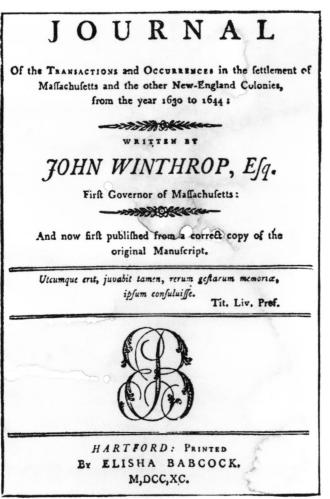

Winthrop's journal was later published.

JOURNAL

Of the TRANSACTIONS and OCCURRENCES in the fettlement of
Maffachufetts and the other New-England Colonies,
from the year 1630 to 1644:

WRITTEN BY

JOHN WINTHROP, Efq.

Firft Governor of Maffachufetts:

And now firft publifhed from a correct copy of the
original Manufcript.

*Utcumque erit, juvabit tamen, rerum geftarum memoriæ,
ipfum confuluiffe.*
Tit. Liv. Præf.

HARTFORD: PRINTED
BY ELISHA BABCOCK.
M,DCC,XC.

evil woman in a Bible story.

The Rev. John Wilson disliked Hutchinson, too. During one sermon, he demanded that she leave the church. Hutchinson stood up with great dignity, turned, and walked out of the church. Her good friend Mary Dyer stood up and walked out also. Dyer

*Sir Henry Vane
(1613–1662)*

was deeply loyal to Hutchinson, who had saved her life by helping her safely deliver a stillborn baby.

Hutchinson had other supporters in Boston. One was Sir Henry Vane, an English statesman who assumed the position of governor for a year. But when he left office, Winthrop was reelected, and that's when Hutchinson's real troubles began.

Winthrop believed that by questioning the authority of those in power, Hutchinson was threatening the security of the colony. This was not acceptable in colonial Massachusetts. Two "troublemakers" had already been removed. The first was Roger Williams, a minister of the church in Salem. Williams had protested against the colonial government because of two principles that he had come to accept. One was that people should have complete religious freedom. The other was that the colonists did not have the right to take land from the Native Americans.

Fearing that these beliefs threatened the security

of Massachusetts Bay Colony, Cotton had asked that a case be brought against Williams. Cotton did not believe that people should have complete religious freedom. "If the people be governors," he asked, "who shall be governed?" He successfully argued against the ideas of Williams, and colonial officials voted to send Williams back to England. Instead, Williams escaped into the wilderness. He received permission from the Native Americans to settle land in what is now Providence, Rhode Island. This became the first North American settlement to allow complete freedom of religion.

Roger Williams built his home in Rhode Island in 1636.

The other "troublemaker" that Winthrop had banished was Hutchinson's brother-in-law, John Wheelwright, who had emigrated in 1636 and held beliefs similar to those of Williams.

Now it was time to deal with Anne Hutchinson.

Winthrop held meetings with Hutchinson and some ministers. He wanted to know whether Hutchinson had criticized their preaching. Cotton stood up for Hutchinson and said she had done nothing wrong. Still, Winthrop decided to bring Hutchinson to trial. He really had no charges against her, but he had a plan.

Most of Hutchinson's supporters lived in Boston. She had few supporters in the other Massachusetts towns. So Winthrop decided to hold the trial in what is now Cambridge. The General Court, which was made up of representatives from all the towns, would hear the case.

The trial began on a cold and windy day in November 1637. An early winter storm had coated the ground with ice, and it was too slippery to ride a horse. Horses were still rare and valued in New England, and owners couldn't risk having a horse fall and break a leg. So, after saying goodbye to her children and leaving young Susanna and William in the care of the older children and the servants, she and her husband bundled up, took a ferry across the Charles River, and walked 5 miles (8 km) to the meetinghouse in Cambridge.

When they opened the door and entered the building, they saw John Winthrop sitting in a chair behind a long table. On benches around the room were the 40 magistrates, or judges. Hutchinson and her supporters had to stand. The room was dark and chilly because it lacked windows and a fireplace.

Winthrop began to question Hutchinson. She answered him cleverly, showing that he had no charges against her. Suddenly, Hutchinson fainted and fell to the floor. As she came to, she realized that she had fainted because she was pregnant. The strain of the day was too much for her body. Winthrop allowed her to sit down, but he kept on with his questioning.

Hutchinson faced her accusers at trial.

Winthrop knew he had to make a legal case. He could not just banish her from the colony. Her supporters in Boston and others in England would strongly object. But he could not show that she was guilty. Even Cotton testified in her favor.

It looked like Hutchinson was going to win. Then, suddenly, she began preaching her understandings of God and Jesus Christ to the ministers and judges. She told them that God had revealed to her that he would punish those who persecuted her. The magistrates and ministers could not believe their ears. Claiming to have revelations from God was unacceptable. They accused her of heresy and banished her from Massachusetts Bay Colony.

If colonists refused to follow the Puritan teachings, they were driven out of Massachusetts Bay Colony.

Through the winter, she was imprisoned in a minister's house. Her younger children, Francis, Samuel, Anne, Mary, Katherine, William, Susanna, and Zuriel, stayed at home with their father. Cousins of Will and some servants helped look after them. Her older children, Edward, Faith, and Bridget, were already married and had homes of their own. They tried to visit their mother as often as they could. However, the winter was very harsh, and the younger children could rarely visit.

In March, she faced a church trial. Her family and friends—including her faithful friend Mary Dyer—turned out to support her. They looked on helplessly as the judges gave her the worst sentence that they could. Hutchinson was excommunicated from the Puritan church, which meant she was no longer considered a member of the church. This time, Cotton had spoken out against her, believing that Hutchinson had gone too far. Wilson delivered the verdict, "I do not only pronounce you worthy to be cast out, but I do cast you out! And in the name of Christ, I do deliver you up to Satan."

Hutchinson stood up and with great dignity walked out of the meetinghouse, hand in hand with Mary Dyer. ✒

8 ANOTHER NEW START

Chapter

❧⟡❧

All winter, while Anne had been imprisoned, Will Hutchinson searched in the wilderness for a new place for them to live. A number of men went along to help with the search. Anne had many followers who no longer wanted to live in Massachusetts. They wanted to follow the Hutchinsons to another place where they could have true religious liberty.

When Roger Williams fled from Salem, he journeyed to land south of Massachusetts. He did not believe that the king of England had a right to grant Indian lands to white settlers. So Williams paid a visit to the Narragansett Indians and offered to buy land from them. The Indians granted him permission to settle along a river that flows into Narragansett Bay. He named his settlement Providence Plantation. In

From the colony's inception, people had religious freedom in Rhode Island. In 1658, 15 Jewish families arrived because Rogers Williams promised that the government would not interfere with their religion. At first, the Jewish congregation worshiped in their homes. In 1763, they built a beautiful house of worship in Newport, the Touro Synagogue. It is the oldest Jewish synagogue in North America.

Providence, people could worship in any manner they wished.

Williams offered to help the Hutchinsons and their followers purchase land along Narragansett Bay. The Indians sold them a place called Aquidneck Island, which later was named Rhode Island. Will and the others began to build houses there.

After Anne's trial was over, she and Will were forced to leave Boston. Once again, Anne and her family left a comfortable home and community because they would not back down from their principles. Her youngest child, Zuriel, was only about 2 years old, and Susanna was only about 5 years old. The Hutchinson family was joined by friends and followers—including Mary Dyer and her husband—as they set off for the new land along Narragansett Bay.

A cold and snowy April made the trip south difficult. They walked for six days, sometimes through thigh-deep snow. Finally, they reached Providence Plantation. Now they believed they had found a place where they could worship as they saw fit.

Anne, Will, and a group of around 65 chose not to

stay in Providence. Instead, they went on to establish what is today Portsmouth, Rhode Island. It took some time to build homes for all the families, so before their houses were finished, they had to live in holes in the ground to keep warm. They placed wooden planks on the bottom of the holes and lined the muddy walls with bark they scraped from tree trunks.

All the while, Hutchinson was feeling sick and weak from her pregnancy. Her head throbbed, and she often threw up her food. Soon she went into early labor and suffered a miscarriage. Hutchinson lost a great deal of blood. For a while, she and her family feared that she would die.

Rhode Island included many small islands. Portsmouth was built on one of these islands.

Mary and Will Dyer followed the Hutchinsons to Rhode Island in 1638. In 1652, the Dyers went back to England, where Mary joined the new Society of Friends, or Quakers. Quakers believed in an "inner light," much as Hutchinson had taught. Mary became a Quaker preacher, and when the Dyers returned to the New World in 1657, she traveled and preached the Quaker beliefs, even in Massachusetts, where it was illegal. These actions led to her being arrested three times and then receiving a death sentence in 1660. She was hanged on June 1, 1660.

Meanwhile back in Boston, Winthrop had received reports of events in Rhode Island. First, he heard there was an earthquake soon after the Hutchinsons arrived. Then he heard about Anne's difficult pregnancy. He reported the rumors that came to him, telling everyone in the colony that she had given birth to 30 monsters. The earthquake and the birth were sure signs that Anne was under the influence of Satan, he said. Winthrop wanted to make sure that Anne would win no more followers from Massachusetts Bay Colony.

Life for the Hutchinsons did not go smoothly in Portsmouth. Quarrels broke out among the settlers. Some of them moved on to found a settlement at what is now Newport, Rhode Island. Then Will Hutchinson died. This was a terrible blow for Anne. She still had young Zuriel, Susanna, William, Katherine, and Anne living at home.

After Will died, Puritan ministers from Massachusetts came to visit Hutchinson in Portsmouth.

They wanted her to repent, admit that she was wrong in her religious beliefs, and return to the Puritan church. Hutchinson refused. Now she no longer felt safe in Portsmouth. She was afraid that Massachusetts would try to take over Rhode Island—and then what would she do? Acting on another revelation from God, Hutchinson decided to take her children and make yet another new start. ℘

Some colonists were locked up in stocks as a punishment for not obeying the laws, while others, like Hutchinson, were banished from the community.

9 HUTCHINSON AND THE INDIANS

Chapter

❧❧❧

Anne Hutchinson tried to think of a place where she would be safe from the Puritans of Massachusetts. She and her older children studied maps and talked about where they might go. They decided to leave the English colonies and traveled to a region called New Netherland, settled by the Dutch. Hutchinson asked the Dutch for permission to settle at what came to be called Pelham Bay. She purchased a piece of land in an area called Vreedelandt, a Dutch word meaning "land of freedom."

In 1609, the Dutch had hired an English explorer named Henry Hudson to look for a northwest passage for ships to sail across North America and reach Asia. Hudson never found such a passage, but he did explore lands around the Hudson River. Because

Anne Hutchinson was saddened by conflicts between colonists and Indians.

of his explorations, the Dutch laid claim to what is now New York, New Jersey, Delaware, and parts of Connecticut, Pennsylvania, and Maryland. They named these lands New Netherland. Dutch traders soon arrived in the New World. The first Dutch settlers began arriving in 1624.

The Dutch claimed land surrounding the Hudson River.

Hutchinson was 51 years old when she moved from Portsmouth to New Netherland. She was joined by 15 others, including servants and seven

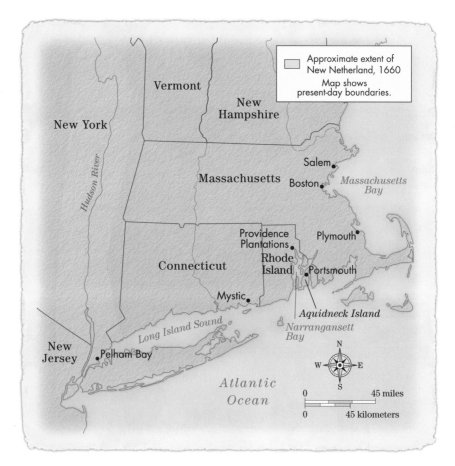

of her children. The group packed up and sent their belongings on ahead of them. Then they traveled by boat from Narragansett Bay to Long Island Sound, passing mainly wilderness areas along the way. They also passed a huge farm that had been settled a few years before by a Scandinavian man named Jonas Bronck. Bronck's farm later came to be called The Bronx, now one of the five boroughs of New York City.

The boats sailed up a small river—which one day would be named the Hutchinson River—to what is now Pelham Bay. The Hutchinson group landed on the shore and declared this was indeed a good place to settle down. Hutchinson and the others went about making a home in New Netherland. At first, the group lived in an abandoned farmhouse. Later, the settlers cut logs and made homes for each family.

There was plenty of food in Pelham Bay. The women and girls made seafood stews from fish the men and boys caught. The men also hunted deer and wild birds. There were even pies made from wild berries the children picked on the hillside. When

> *Hutchinson had five grown children who did not join her in New Netherland. Her oldest sons, Edward and Richard, lived in Boston. A daughter, Faith, and her husband and son lived in what is now Braintree, Massachusetts. Another daughter, Bridget, remained in Rhode Island with her husband and sons. Samuel, who was 17 years old, also chose to stay in Rhode Island.*

spring came in 1643, Hutchinson planted an herb garden so that she could make her medicines.

Hutchinson continued to study the Bible and think about God. The only people she could teach and preach to were the members of her little colony. Hutchinson had only a few Dutch neighbors, and none of them spoke English. The Dutch were very tolerant of other religions, so Hutchinson thought that she and her group would be safe. There was one big problem, however. The Dutch and the local Native Americans did not get along.

The Algonquian and the Iroquois were the main Native American groups in the area. At the time Hutchinson arrived, the tribes were at war with one another. Willem Kieft, the leader of the Dutch colony, sold weapons to both sides. He angered them when he demanded that the Native Americans pay him a tribute of corn and beads called wampum, to signify the submission of the Indians to the Dutchman.

Other Dutch settlers upset the Native Americans by allowing their cattle and pigs to roam around the Indians' farm fields and eat their

Battles between the Algonquian and Iroquois tribes were largely over the rights to land and hunting. Fur trade had become important to the Indians and they wanted to make sure they had land filled with pelt-bearing animals. The series of battles became known as the Beaver Wars, after the much-wanted fur of the beaver.

corn. The native people then strained relations further when they killed and ate the roaming livestock. The angry settlers warned Hutchinson to be leery of the Indians and to keep guns in the house for defense.

Indians and Dutch merchants trade on Manhattan Island during the 1600s.

But Hutchinson refused. She said that she had nothing to fear from the Native Americans because they had nothing to fear from her.

Hutchinson, like Roger Williams, did not believe that rulers in Europe had a right to give away land to white settlers in America. The land belonged to the Native Americans. Hutchinson believed that the Native Americans should be treated with respect.

Her views on Native Americans had angered Governor Winthrop when she lived in Massachusetts Bay Colony. Winthrop and other Puritans believed that the native people were heathens and controlled by Satan. He believed that God had given Puritans the right to take their land and that the Puritans had a duty to convert them to Christianity.

The Massachusetts Bay Colony was in conflict with a tribe called the Pequot. The Pequot lived in what is now the southern part of Connecticut. Seeking more land, some Puritans from Massachusetts had settled in this area. There had been arguments over land and trading rights among the Pequot, the Narragansett, and the white settlers since the early 1630s.

One of the first conflicts between the Puritans and the Pequot occurred in 1634 when members of the Pequot killed a dishonest English trader and his crew. The Puritans wanted the Pequot to punish the men who had killed the trader, but the Indians refused. They claimed that the Englishmen had kidnapped some tribal members to hold them for ransom.

Then in 1636, a colonial officer was killed at what is now Block Island, Rhode Island. The Puritans accused the Pequot of the murder and sent troops to punish them. The Native Americans escaped, but the angry Puritan soldiers burned and looted their village. In revenge, the Pequot attacked the

Puritan settlements in Connecticut.

The leaders of the Massachusetts Bay Colony then formed an alliance with another native tribe called the Mohegan and declared war on the Pequot. In May 1637, the Puritans and the Mohegan attacked a Pequot village in the early dawn near what is now Mystic, Connecticut. They set fire to the wigwams where the Pequot lay asleep. When the fighting was over, between 400 and 700 Pequot men, women, and children were dead. Any Pequot that remained alive were sent to Bermuda and sold into slavery.

A 19th-century illustration of the Pequot massacre in 1637

Hutchinson had opposed the war and was horrified at the massacre. When she moved to Portsmouth, she had become friends with the local Narragansett. Hutchinson thought she would also be friends with the Native Americans in her New Netherland home.

Serious trouble broke out in 1643 between Dutch settlers and Native Americans. A tribe of Algonquian, who were fleeing from an Iroquois tribe, thought they would be safe in Dutch territory and set up camp on Manhattan Island. Willem Kieft, however, thought the Indians were planning an uprising, so he sent Dutch soldiers to kill them. More than 100 men, women, and children were killed. All the Algonquian tribes in the area vowed revenge, including a group called the Siwanoy.

The Algonquian began their attacks on the Dutch of New Netherland in August. Hutchinson's Dutch neighbors warned her that the Siwanoy were coming. They told her to take her small colony and "disappear." But Hutchinson refused to leave her home. She even refused to arm herself, her servants, or her family members. Trusting in God's protection, she thought she had nothing to fear. After all, she had nothing to do with the attacks on the Algonquian. She and the Native Americans had always gotten along very well.

August 20, 1643, was a clear, beautiful day. A chief named Wampage led the Siwanoy war party up a hill on Pelham Bay to a small settlement. He was no doubt surprised to find Hutchinson and her family at home. The family showed no fear of him or his warriors. He asked them to tie up the family dogs, which they did. Then quickly,

The Algonquian had been sleeping when the Dutch settlers attacked their camp.

Six of Anne Hutchinson's children died alongside her.

the warriors grabbed Hutchinson and her family members, killed them, and cut off their scalps. They dragged the bodies into a house and burned it to the ground.

One of Hutchinson's daughters escaped, however. Nine-year-old Susanna had gone off to pick blueberries some distance away from the houses. According to legend, she hid in the crack of a boulder after she heard the screams of her family and saw smoke from the burning house. When the Siwanoy found her, they likely realized they had made a mistake. They had not killed a Dutch family. They had killed the English family of Anne Hutchinson.

Wampage took Susanna captive and later adopted her as his own daughter. She lived with the Siwanoy until she was about 18 years old. She then went to Boston and married a man named John Cole. They had 11 children. Susanna died in 1713 at the age of 80. ✲

10 A LEGACY OF LIBERTY

❦

The story of Anne Hutchinson does not end with her death. Her fame began to grow, and she became recognized as a woman of great faith and courage. But her legacy is filled with questionable interpretations of who she was.

Both in her life and her death, Anne Hutchinson has been described as something she was not. When she was alive, her enemies accused her of spreading "abominable wickedness" when she shared views that differed from theirs. Today, she is often portrayed as a feminist and a champion of religious freedom. But there are no written records to prove she was either of these things. What we do know is that Hutchinson protested her government because she had a great faith that her beliefs were good and true.

A statue of Anne Hutchinson stands outside the Boston State House.

Religious persecution led an English Quaker named William Penn to found a Quaker colony in 1681 in what is now Pennsylvania. Quakers and others who were persecuted for their religion went to live there. Penn's colony was another place that guaranteed freedom of religion.

After Hutchinson was killed, leaders in Boston saw her murder as a just end for a troublemaker. Winthrop wrote about the conflict with Anne Hutchinson, and about the woman herself:

This American Jezebel kept her strength and reputation, even among the people of God, till the hand of civil justice laid hold on her, and then she began evidently to decline, ... God giving her up since the sentence of excommunication, to that hardness of heart, as she is not affected with any remorse, but glories in it, and fears not the vengeance of God, which she lies under, as if God did work contrary to his own word ...

Eventually Massachusetts honored Hutchinson. Outside the State House in Boston, a statue erected in 1923 reminds visitors of her great contributions to freedom. A plaque on the statue reads:

In memory of Anne Marbury Hutchinson, baptized at Alford, Lincolnshire, England, 20-July 1591, killed by the Indians at East Chester, New York, 1643. Courageous exponent of civil liberty and religious toleration.

In 1987, Michael Dukakis, then governor of Massachusetts, formally pardoned Hutchinson, and the banishment ordered by Governor Winthrop was at last officially revoked.

Other honors to Hutchinson are found throughout the areas where she lived. New York honored her in the 1920s by giving a new road that was built along the Hutchinson River the name of Hutchinson River Parkway.

Hutchinson's legacy also includes her descendants, many of whom have played important roles in U.S. history. Some became governors of Rhode Island and Massachusetts, and three distant grandsons even became U.S. presidents.

President Franklin Delano Roosevelt (1882–1945)

Franklin Delano Roosevelt was president from 1933 to 1945; George Herbert Walker Bush, from 1989 to 1993; and George Walker Bush, who became president in 2001. First lady Eleanor Roosevelt, one of the most admired women of the 20th century, named Hutchinson as one of the women she admired most.

One of Hutchinson's important contributions was to help found the state of Rhode Island. Providence, Portsmouth, Newport, and another settlement called Warwick joined together under one charter in 1647. Rhode Island became a state in 1790, after the American Revolutionary

Because of its tolerance, Rhode Island has long been a home to people of many religions. The Jewish Touro Synagogue was dedicated in 1762 in Newport.

War. From its beginnings, Rhode Island was known as a place of religious tolerance. Baptists, Quakers, other Christian sects, and Jews were welcomed there.

Perhaps Anne Hutchinson's most important contribution, however, was her willingness to stand up for the principles she believed in. Complete religious freedom was a new idea in the 1600s, but today Americans consider it a basic human right. ❧

HUTCHINSON'S LIFE

1605

Moves to London with her family after her father gets a teaching position there

1591

Baptized in July in Alford, England

1590

1600

1597

The great English scientist Francis Bacon publishes *Essays, Civil and Moral*

1603

James I becomes king of England and Ireland

WORLD EVENTS

1612

Marries William Hutchinson and moves to Alford; John Cotton begins preaching at St. Boltoph's in Boston, England

1611

Her father, Francis Marbury, dies

1610

1607

Jamestown, Virginia, the first English settlement on the North American mainland, is founded

1611

The King James Bible, commissioned by the British king, is published

HUTCHINSON'S LIFE

1613

Gives birth to the first
of 15 children

1630

The plague strikes
Alford, killing two of
Anne Hutchinson's
daughters

1630

1614

Pocahontas marries
John Rolfe

1628

John Bunyan,
popular English
author, is born

WORLD EVENTS

1632

Is saddened when
Cotton and eldest
son, Edward,
leave England for
Massachusetts
Bay Colony

1634

Sails to Boston,
Massachusetts; begins
holding religious
meetings in her home

1635

1632

King Charles I issues
a charter for the
colony of Maryland

1634

Jean Nicolet lands
on Green Bay and
explores what is now
Wisconsin

1635

English High and
Latin School, Boston,
Massachusetts,
oldest secondary
school in North
America, is founded

HUTCHINSON'S LIFE

1637

Tried for heresy,
found guilty,
and banished

1638

Moves to Rhode
Island; suffers a
miscarriage

1636

Harvard College
founded at
Cambridge,
Massachusetts

1638

Louis XIV, future king
of France, is born

WORLD EVENTS

1643

Hutchinson and six children are killed by a war party of Native Americans

1641

William Hutchinson dies

1640

1640

The *Bay Psalm Book* is the first book printed in British North America

1642

Isaac Newton, English mathematician and philosopher, is born

FULL NAME: Anne Marbury Hutchinson

DATE OF BIRTH: July 1591

PLACE OF BIRTH: Alford, England

FATHER: Francis Marbury
(1555–1611)

MOTHER: Bridget Dryden
(1563?–1645)

SPOUSE: William Hutchinson
(1586–1641)

DATE OF MARRIAGE: August 9, 1612

CHILDREN: Edward (1613–1675)
Susanna (1614?–1630)
Richard (1615?–?)
Faith (1617?–1651)
Bridget (1618?–1698)
Francis (1620?–1643)
Elizabeth (1622?–1630)
William (1623?–1624?)
Samuel (1624–?)
Anne (1626?–1643)
Mary (1628?–1643)
Katherine (1630?–1643)
William (1631?–1643)
Susanna (1633–1713)
Zuriel (1636?–1643)

DATE OF DEATH: August 20, 1643

PLACE OF DEATH: Pelham Bay, New York

FURTHER READING

Clark, Beth, Arthur M. Schlesinger, and Arthur M. Schlesinger Jr. *Anne Hutchinson: Religious Leader.* New York: Chelsea House, 2000.

Kent, Deborah. *In Colonial New England.* New York: Benchmark Books, 1999.

Levy, Elizabeth, and Daniel McFeeley (illustrator). *Cranky Colonials: Pilgrims, Puritans 1560s–1740s.* New York: Scholastic, 2003.

Nichols, Joan Kane, and Dan Krovatin (illustrator). *A Matter of Conscience: The Trial of Anne Hutchinson.* Austin, Tex.: Steck-Vaughn, 1992.

LOOK FOR MORE SIGNATURE LIVES BOOKS ABOUT THIS ERA:

Lord Baltimore: *Founder of Maryland*
ISBN 0-7565-1592-0

William Penn: *Founder of Pennsylvania*
ISBN 0-7565-1598-X

Roger Williams: *Founder of Rhode Island*
ISBN 0-7565-1596-3

John Winthrop: *First Governor of Massachusetts*
ISBN 0-7565-1591-2

ON THE WEB

For more information on *Anne Hutchinson*, use FactHound.

1. Go to *www.facthound.com*
2. Type in a search word related to this book or this book ID: 076515777
3. Click on the *Fetch It* button.

FactHound will fetch Web sites related to this book.

HISTORIC SITES

Massachusetts State House
Beacon Street at Park Street
Boston, Massachusetts
617/727-3676
A statue of Anne Hutchinson stands outside the west wing of the building

Founders Brook Park
Off Boyd's Lane
Portsmouth, Rhode Island
Site where Anne Hutchinson and her group of settlers landed in Portsmouth

Glossary

charter
a written grant of rights to a colony

dissent
to disagree with the opinion of others

grace
God's divine love

heresy
a religious belief that is different from those accepted by a church

legacy
gift passed on by someone who has died

Reformation
a religious movement in the Catholic Church in the 1500s that led to the founding of Protestant churches

revelations
the presentations of truths directly from God

statesman
a leader in national or international affairs

wampum
small beads strung together in designs to record events; sometimes used as money

wigwams
bark huts used by Native Americans

Chapter 1

Page 10, line 20: Eve La Plante. *American Jezebel: The Uncommon Life of Anne Hutchinson, the Woman Who Defied the Puritans.* San Francisco: HarperSanFrancisco, 2004, p. 2.

Chapter 2

Page 16, line 20: Ibid., p. 23.

Chapter 4

Page 31, line 13: Ibid., p. 85.

Chapter 5

Page 43, sidebar: Eric B. Schultz. "Aboard the Griffin." *Cobblestone* November 2003: 18-21.

Page 45, line 5: Duane A. Cline. "Voyage of the *Mayflower*." *The Pilgrims and Plymouth Colony: 1620.* 26 Oct. 2005. www.rootsweb.com/~mosmd/index.htm.

Page 47, line 6: *American Jezebel: The Uncommon Life of Anne Hutchinson, the Woman Who Defied the Puritans*, p. 63.

Page 47, line 9: Ibid., p. 64.

Page 47, line 23: Ibid.

Page 48, line 3: Ibid.

Page 49, line 9: Ibid., p. 65.

Chapter 6

Page 59, sidebar: Ibid.,p. 99.

Page 60, line 8: Jay Rogers. "America's Christian Leaders: Anne Hutchinson." 21 March 2005. www.forerunner.com/forerunner/X0193_Anne_Hutchinson.html.

Page 61, line 3: *American Jezebel: The Uncommon Life of Anne Hutchinson, the Woman Who Defied the Puritans*, p. 55.

Chapter 7

Page 64, line 24: "Women of the Hall: Anne Hutchinson." National Women's Hall of Fame 10 November 2005. www.greatwomen.org/women.php?action=viewone&id=84.

Page 64, line 28: *American Jezebel: The Uncommon Life of Anne Hutchinson, the Woman Who Defied the Puritans*, p. xvii.

Page 67, line 4: "John Cotton, Letter to Lord Say and Sele (1636)." The Pragmatism Cybrary. 10 Nov. 2005. www.pragmatism.org/american/docs/cotton_letter.htm.

Page 71, line 21: *American Jezebel: The Uncommon Life of Anne Hutchinson, the Woman Who Defied the Puritans*, p. 204.

Chapter 10

Page 92, line 7: Ibid., pp. 244–245.

Page 92, line 24: Marjorie Alsing Trimble. "Three Women of Courage." The Family Stories Project of the Wilbraham Public Library. 26 Oct. 2005. www.wilbrahamlibrary.org/about/family stories/margorie%20trimble/plaque.jpg.

Anne Hutchinson. 2 Oct. 2005. www.annehutchinson.com.

Boorstin, Daniel J. *The Americans: The Colonial Experience.* New York: Vintage Books, 1964.

Boorstin, Daniel J. *The Americans: The National Experience.* New York: Vintage Books, 1965.

Earle, Alice Morse. *Home Life in Colonial Days.* Stockbridge, Mass.: Berkshire Traveller Press, 1974.

James, Edward T., ed. *Notable American Women: 1607-1950.* Cambridge, Mass.: Belkamp Press, 1971.

Kerber, Linda K., and Jane Sherron De Hart, eds. *Women's America: Refocusing the Past.* New York: Oxford University Press, 1995.

LaPlante, Eve. *American Jezebel: The Uncommon Life of Anne Hutchinson, the Woman Who Defied the Puritans.* San Francisco: HarperSanFrancisco, 2004.

May, Roy H., Jr. "Manifest Destiny: America the New Israel." *Joshua and the Promised Land.* 5 Oct. 2005. http://gbgm-umc.org/umw/joshua/manifest.html.

McHenry, Robert, ed. *Famous American Women: A Biographical Dictionary from Colonial Times to the Present.* New York: Dover, 1980.

Mrs. Anne Hutchinson: Trial at the Court at Newton. 1637. 5 Oct. 2005. www.piney-2.com/ColAnnHutchTrial.html.

A Puritan's Mind. 5 Oct. 2005. www.apuritansmind.com.

Rugg, Winnifred King. *Unafraid: A Life of Anne Hutchinson.* Boston: Houghton Mifflin, 1930. Questia: The World's Largest Online Library. www.questia.com/PM.qst?a=o&d=6310583.

Alford, England, 15, 16, 17, 26–27, 31, 36, 37, 38
Algonquian Indians, 82, 86
Anglican Church. *See* Church of England.
Antinomians, 64
Aquidneck Island, 74

Beaver Wars, 82
Bible, 10, 12, 21, 26, 29, 35, 36, 46, 53, 56–57, 59, 63, 82
Bilsby, England, 36, 38
Black Death, 37
Block Island, Rhode Island, 84
Boleyn, Anne, 25, 28
Boston, England, 32, 33, 36
Boston, Massachusetts, 49, 51–52, 53, 54, 57–58, 61, 68, 76, 81, 89, 92
Braintree, Massachusetts, 81
Bronck, Jonas, 81
The Bronx, 81
Bush, George Herbert Walker, 93
Bush, George Walker, 93

Cambridge, Massachusetts, 52, 53, 68, 69
Cambridge University, 15, 29, 32
Catherine of Aragon, 24, 25
Charles I, king of England, 53
Charles River, 68
charter, 53, 64
Church of England, 11, 15, 16–17, 25–26, 38, 45
Cole, John, 89
Cotton, John, 32–34, 35, 36–37, 38, 41, 49, 58–59, 60, 64, 67, 68, 70, 71

Dukakis, Michael, 93
Dutch settlers, 54, 79–80, 82–83, 86
Dyer, Mary, 65–66, 71, 74, 76
Dyer, Will, 76

Edward VI, king of England, 25
"the elect," 55–56, 59–60, 61
Elizabeth I, queen of England, 25

Elizabethan Age, 25

fens, 16
First Church of Boston, 51, 58, 59
France, 64

General Court, 10, 68
Globe theater, 28, 29
Great Britain, 11, 21, 23, 24, 25, 29, 37
Griffin (ship), 38, 41, 43, 47, 49

Henry VIII, king of England, 23–25
Holland, 11–12, 38, 45
Holy Communion, 26
Howland, John, 45
Hudson, Henry, 79–80
Hudson River, 79
Hutchinson, Anne
    banishment of, 12, 71, 74
    birth of, 15, 18
    birthname of, 15
    childhood of, 18, 19–20, 26
    children of, 34, 36, 37–38, 38–39, 68, 71, 74, 76, 80–81, 88–89
    death of, 88
    descendents of, 93
    education of, 20–21
    health of, 69, 75
    imprisonment of, 71
    John Cotton and, 31–32, 32–33, 34, 35–36, 36–37, 38, 49, 58–59, 68, 70, 71
    John Winthrop and, 9, 10, 57, 60–61, 64–65, 68, 69–70, 76, 92
    journey to New Netherland, 80–81
    journey to New World, 41, 43, 46–47
    journey to Providence Plantation, 74
    marriage of, 31
    meetings of, 10, 36, 37, 59, 60, 63, 64
    as midwife, 35, 58, 66

Darlene R. Stille is the author of more than 80 books for young people, including collections of biographies. She grew up in Chicago and attended the University of Illinois, where she discovered her love of writing. She now lives and writes in Michigan.

Image Credits